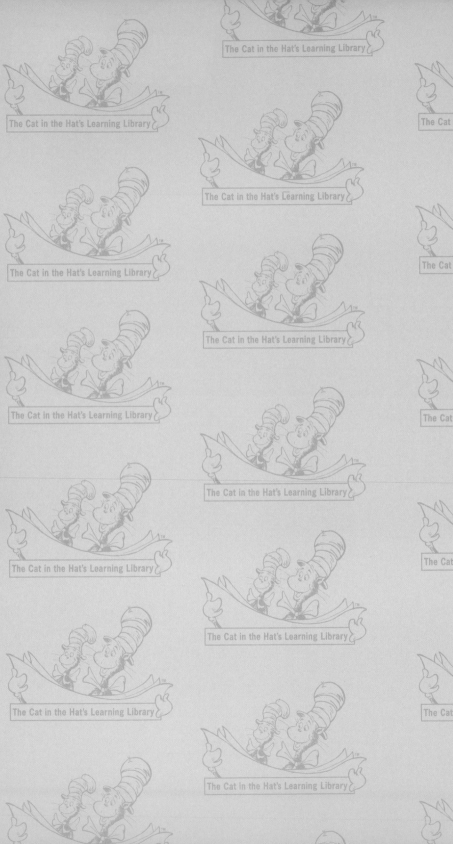

The editors would like to thank
BARBARA KIEFER, Ph.D.,
Charlotte S. Huck Professor of Children's Literature,
The Ohio State University, and
JIM BREHENY, Director, Bronx Zoo Special Animal Exhibits and Operations,
Wildlife conservation Society,
for their assistance in the preparation of this book.

First published in the UK by HarperCollins Children's Books in 2008
12

ISBN: 978 0 00 797524 2

Printed in China by RR Donnelley APS

IF I RAN THE RAINFOREST

by Bonnie Worth

illustrated by Aristides Ruiz

The Cat in the Hat's Learning Library™

HarperCollins *Children's Books*

I'm the Cat in the Hat
and it's time that we get
to go to a place
that is steamy and wet.

It is a rainforest.

The reason is clear.

About one hundred inches

of rain falls each year.

Down at the equator

I'll show it to you.

Your mother won't mind

very much if I do.

EQUATOR

RAINFOREST

BRAZIL

To a tropical rainforest
off we will go!
There are three other kinds
I think you should know.

The seasonal kind
has months that are dry.
A cloud rainforest
sits three thousand feet high.

A mangrove rainforest
grows on the coast.
Rain falls on the tropical
rainforest most.

Dear Sally and Nick,
for your information,
the reason it's rainy
is called tran-spi-ra-tion.

TRANSPIRATION

- Plants lose water through pores in their leaves.

- Warm, wet air rises into the sky.

- Wet air cools and forms rain clouds.

- Plants soak up rain through their roots.

A rainforest has
four floors, you might say.
We'll visit each one,
so please step this way.

My umbrella-vator
will give the best view.
To the uppermost floor
it will take me and you.

12

E-mer-gents is the word
that we use to call
these trees that grow up
three hundred feet tall.

They might be quite tall,
but I'm here to report
their roots don't go deep,
but they still give support.

Buttress roots grow
above ground like a fan
to keep trees from falling.
That is Nature's plan.

Who makes their home here?
Those who like heights best . . .

Buttress
roots

. . . an eagle named harpy
here makes her high nest.

This gaggle of parrots
of colourful hue
are macaws of scarlet
and yellow and blue.

Now we will go
down to floor three,
where lower treetops
form the green canopy.

It keeps rain and sun
off the floors down below.
It's also the place where
the e-pi-phytes grow.

These plants have roots
that hang here and there.
They suck up the moisture
right out of the air!

TOUCANS

The canopy is
the most crowded of spots.
Here monkeys and tree frogs
and birds can eat lots
of fruits, nuts and bugs
and the nectar of flowers.

ORCHIDS

TREE FROGS

It is NOISY round here,
and it's busy all hours!

Some animals here,
I have just found,
live their whole lives
without touching the ground!

RED-EYED
TREE FROGS

The wet leaves are slippy.
Movement is tricky.
And that's why their toes
and their fingers are sticky.

In the canopy – hark!
The hummingbirds hum.
Over two hundred kinds.
That is quite a large sum!

The hummingbird sips
at the nectar from blooms.
From flower to flower,
it flits and it zooms.

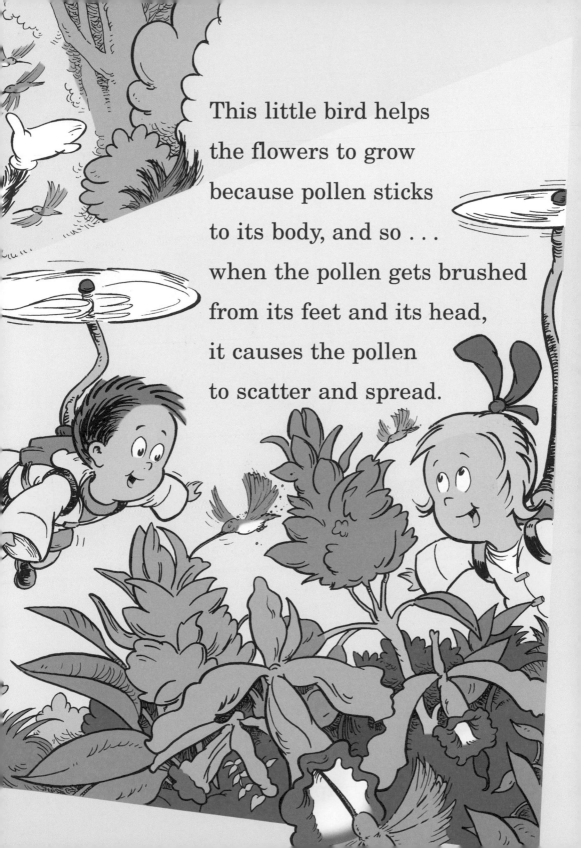

This little bird helps
the flowers to grow
because pollen sticks
to its body, and so . . .
when the pollen gets brushed
from its feet and its head,
it causes the pollen
to scatter and spread.

pitcher plants

This plant gives an insect
a most deadly ride.
It slips when it sips
and gets trapped inside.

strangler fig

If this plant can't root,
it will grow on another.
The vines twine and squeeze
and then, finally, smother!

The under canopy is
the next stop: floor two.
I'm afraid not much sun
can make its way through.

These vines and ferns grow
where it's dim and it's hot.
Spider monkey lives here,
and the wild ocelot.

Cam-ou-flage is the word
to describe a design
that makes things blend in
and so hard to find.

Find six hidden things
and you'll win a prize.
The sure way to win
is to sharpen your eyes.

31

Last stop: the first floor.
The doors open wide.
And when we look out,
it is quite dark outside!

Is anyone home?
At first, you'd say not.
There's mostly leaf litter,
dead plants and some rot.

But jaguars prowl,
snakes slink and they slither.
Insects and spiders
creep yon and hither.

Now look even closer
and you will find
among the life here . . .

. . . is our own humankind!

For thousands of years,
they've lived here unharmed.
They've hunted and some
of them even have farmed.

They know where to find
the food for a meal.
They know which plants poison.
They know which plants heal.

You've seen all four floors.
See if you can list them.
These four floors make up
a complete ecosystem.

howler monkeys

harpy eagles

mac

ocelots

snakes

kinkajous

But something has happened
within recent years.
A thing that is going to
drive me to tears.

jaguars

centipedes

eaglets

Millions of acres
of land every year
are cut down for reasons
too long to list here.

spider monkeys

toucans

sloths

native human

If I ran the rain forest,
you know what I'd do?
I'd make a few changes.
That's just what I'd do.

I'd say, "Chop somewhere else, people. Leave us these trees. Don't cut them down."

"Save these trees, please!"

GLOSSARY

Acre: A piece of land that was originally equal to the area that a team of oxen could plough in one day. An acre is about the size of a football field.

Buttress: To support or hold up.

Camouflage: To hide by blending in or being disguised.

Ecosystem: A group of animals and plants that live together.

Emergent: A tall tree that pokes through the forest canopy.

Epiphyte: An air plant that thrives on the branches or trunk of another plant.

Equator: An imaginary circle running around the earth that lies an equal distance from the North and South Poles.

Hither and yon: An old-time way to say "here and there".

Hue: A shade of colour.

Nectar: The sweet liquid found inside flowers, which bees use to make honey.

Pollen: The fine dust found inside flowers, which helps them reproduce new flowers.

Smother: To stop a living thing from breathing by covering or strangling.

Transpiration: The process in which plants lose water through pores in their leaves called "stomata". As water is lost from the plant, the plant takes up more water through its roots.

FOR FURTHER READING

The Rainforest at Night by Nic Bishop (Collins Educational).
Meet the animals and insects that live in the rainforest.
By award-winning wildlife photographer, Nic Bishop.
For ages 4+ (978-0-00-723605-3).

Cloud Forest by Nic Bishop (Collins Educational). A photographic
exploration of one of the world's most beautiful type of rainforest.
For ages 4+ (978-0-00-718641-9).

24 Hours: Rainforest (Dorling Kindersley). Go around the clock
with the spectacular animals of the rainforest. For ages 5+.

Eye Wonder: Rainforest (Dorling Kindersley). Filled with
fascinating facts and dramatic photography. For ages 5+.

INDEX

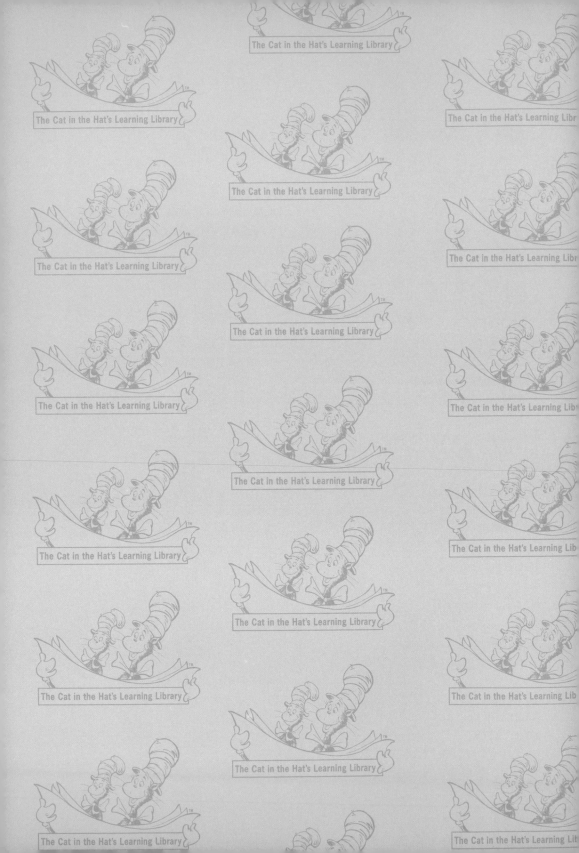

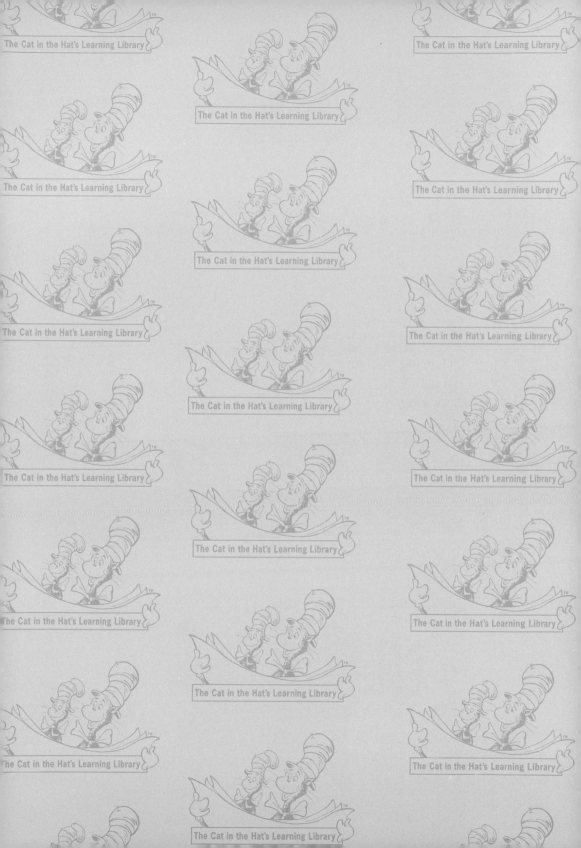

If you love The Cat in the Hat
then look out for these great titles to collect:

OH SAY CAN YOU SAY WHAT'S THE WEATHER TODAY

WOULD YOU RATHER BE A TADPOLE?

MY OH MY A BUTTERFLY

I CAN NAME 50 TREES TODAY

MILES AND MILES OF REPTILES

A GREAT DAY FOR PUP

CLAM-I-AM!

A WHALE OF A TALE!

THERE'S NO PLACE LIKE SPACE!

OH, THE PETS YOU CAN GET!

IF I RAN THE RAIN FOREST

INSIDE YOUR OUTSIDE!

FINE FEATHERED FRIENDS

OH, THE THINGS YOU CAN DO THAT ARE GOOD FOR YOU!

IS A CAMEL A MAMMAL?

WISH FOR A FISH

OH SAY CAN YOU SAY DI-NO-SAUR?

ON BEYOND BUGS

OH SAY CAN YOU SEED?